What Leaders Do

A Leadership Primer

What Leaders Do

A Leadership Primer

Dave Browning

prim·er *n*

1. a book used to teach young children to read, typically containing simple stories
2. a book that provides an introduction to a topic
3. somebody or something that primes something

lead·er *n*

1. a person who sees what needs to be done
2. a person who does what needs to be done

iUniverse, Inc.
New York   Bloomington

What Leaders Do
A Leadership Primer

Copyright © 2009 by Dave Browning

Universe books may be ordered through booksellers or by contacting:

iUniverse
1663 Liberty Drive
Bloomington, IN 47403
www.iuniverse.com
1-800-Authors (1-800-288-4677)

ISBN: 978-0-595-53301-5 (pbk)
ISBN: 978-0-595-63356-2 (ebk)

Printed in the United States of America

iUniverse rev. date: 5/04/2008

Contents

Introduction

EVERYTHING rises and falls with leadership. You cannot go from "in the beginning" to "happily ever after" outside the influence of a leader. And extremely happy endings don't involve just one strong leader, but many at all levels.

What do leaders do? My answer is fairly simple. In short, leaders see what needs to be done, and they do what needs to be done. It doesn't sound like much, but actually that's saying a lot.

Leaders come in all shapes and sizes. Some are bold in their style, some are unassuming. Some fly by the seat of their pants. Some are very calculating. Even the Apostles of Jesus varied greatly in their approaches to leadership. Peter was a powerhouse. James was a practical tactician. John was a lover. Yet they all made an impact. They saw what needed to be done, and they did what needed to be done.

Are leaders made, or born? Leaders are made. Of course, they are born first. Then most of it is education, experience and emphasis. It is nature and nurture. But regardless of how they came to do so, leaders end up leading. In the end, they get something done.

"Done" is a word that indicates change in the environment from pre-leadership to post-leadership. If things are still the same as they were, then nothing's been done. If nothing's been done, leadership has not been exercised. Leaders change things. They alter the state of things. They leave a mark.

There is much being written these days about collaboration and teamwork. Truly, there is nothing more exciting than seeing a group of people accomplish something extraordinary. But make no mistake - there are no great teams out there without great coaches. Leadership is to a group what spark is to a flame.

One of my earliest memories helped me define leadership. The little Alaskan church I attended as a boy called a new pastor after a protracted vacancy. The church lacked morale and momentum. We were occupying a half-finished church building, having run out of funds to complete the project. The surroundings were crude – floors without carpets, unfinished walls, rudimentary furnishings. Our numbers were small. But the first action of the new pastor put in motion a virtuous cycle. He removed the makeshift communion table (a flimsy garage sale castoff) from the front of the church and raised money for a solid, wooden one. It was a symbolic act, but a powerful one. As a boy looking on, this made quite an impression on me. It was a microcosm of leadership. He saw what needed to be done and he did what needed to be done.

In *What Leaders Do* I am going to unpack the specifics of "the seeing" that leaders see, and "the doing" that leaders do. While this book won't make you a leader, it will give you a track to run on if you want to be one.

The subject of leadership is multi-faceted. You can approach it from several angles, including:

- Character

- Vision

- Communication

- Management

- Teamwork

While each aspect of leadership deserves individual investigation, *What Leaders Do* is a prequel to help you see "the bigger picture" – the forest instead of the trees. The sections of *What Leaders Do* develop the two major functionalities of leadership:

1. Leaders See What Needs To Be Done

   a. They Define Reality

   b. They Envision a Preferable Future

2. Leaders Do What Needs To Be Done

   a. They Enlist Others

   b. They Follow Through

The four sub-sections roughly correspond to the survey results of Kouzes and Posner that became of the basis of their book *The Leadership Challenge*. From over 20,000 questionnaires, administered twice, they gleaned four qualities considered most important in leaders: Honesty, Forward-Looking, Inspiring, Competent. *What Leaders Do* focuses on the behaviors that emanate from these qualities.

Qualities	Behaviors
Honesty	They Define Reality
Forward-Looking	They Envision a Preferable Future
Inspiring	They Enlist Others
Competent	They Follow Through

The scarcest resource in the world today is leadership talent. There is an unlimited supply of great opportunities, but a limited supply of great people. We need leaders everywhere – education, politics, health care. But I am particularly eager for you to hone your leadership if you are a minister of Jesus Christ, concerned with advancing his agenda. E.M. Bounds notes that while the Church might be searching for better methods, "God is searching for better men."

At Christ the King Community Church (CTK), where I function as a leader, our mission is *to create an authentic Christian community that effectively reaches out to unchurched people with love, acceptance and forgiveness so that they may experience the joy of salvation and a purposeful life of discipleship.* Our vision is *to see a prevailing, multi-location church emerge that will transform the spiritual landscape. This church will convene in thousands of small groups with Worship Centers strategically located in every community.* These are leadership-dependent propositions. When you organize by small groups, you need a leader for every ten people. When you decentralize into many Worship Centers, you need a leader for every community. The leadership challenge has become so clear to us that we have concluded that we are not actually in the church business. **We are in the leader business**.

The church of Jesus Christ holds the hope of the world in its hands and is the most leadership intensive enterprise in society. We need you. We really do. God may call you to be a leader in another context, but in whatever context you are placed, please "Go for it." Do not limit your thinking. Expand your vision. Be aggressive. See what needs to be done. Do what needs to be done. Everything rises and falls with leadership.

(For ease in writing I have used masculine pronouns throughout. It should be understood that the principles described here apply to men and women.)

Leaders See What Needs to Be Done

LEADERS possess acuity, a power of observation that sets them apart. Leaders see what others cannot readily see, and in greater clarity. They see both the problems and the possibilities. While others are complacent or despondent (stuck in "quo or wo"), leaders are homing in on what needs to be done, and saying, "Let's change this."

A leader can see both what is, and what could be. And in between the reality and the possibilities they can also see what it takes to get there from here. There are some people who can see what is, but not what could be. We might call these folks "concerned individuals" but not leaders. There are other people who can see what could be, but cannot clarify the obstacles that prevent us from getting there. We might call these folks "dreamers" but not leaders. Leaders see where we are, where we need to go, and how to get there.

1

They Define Reality

LEADERS begin by defining current reality. According to Max DePree, the author of *Leadership is an Art,* this is the first responsibility for a leader, to define reality. **Leaders size up the situation as it really is**. The role of a leader is to help people face reality and then mobilize them to make a change. But a leader cannot help others face reality until he has done so himself. Facing reality sounds simple, but it is actually hard to see a situation for what it is and not for what it was, or what you wish it to be.

For some, defining reality is an acquired skill. But when a person has a leadership gift, defining reality is nearly involuntary. Gifted leaders cannot walk into any establishment without thinking about how the presentation could be made better. They critique news anchors for diction, paperboys for newspaper placement, restaurants for decor, and coaches for plays. And a leader can't turn it off when he goes to church, as Bill Hybels says in *Rediscovering Church*:

> When a person with a leadership gift walks around
> the church, mental warning buzzers go off all over the
> place. His or her mind is racing with thoughts like "We
> need to pay more attention to this" and "We need to
> solve that," and "We need to get this back on track,"
> and "We've got to figure out why we're still doing this
> when it's no longer working" and "We've got to start
> a new program to accomplish something else."

Great leaders size up situations quickly. In the military, brilliant leaders are said to possess "coup d'oeil" – which in French means "the power of the glance." They immediately get a feeling for what's going on. Particularly, they evaluate what's going on in four realms:

What's going on in the world?

LEADERS are broadly interested. They are inquisitive on a variety of topics. They **listen and learn so they can link and lead**. Leaders are often avid readers because reading gives them the benefit of organized thought (someone can speak without thinking, but they cannot write without thinking).

Leaders find out what's going on, not just on the surface level, but in the grander scheme of things. Leaders look beyond mere circumstance for cause and effect, patterns and cycles. They track trends. They have the pulse of things. They know what's happening on a macro scale.

What's going on in Christ's kingdom?

IN addition to seeing the bigger picture, Christian leaders also "see" unseen realities and agendas. They pay attention to the much-bigger picture, what theologians have called the meta-narrative. The meta-narrative is the story of God's eventual redemption of his fallen planet. In moments when smaller stories do not make sense, a leader keeps in mind the over-arching story, the redemptive plan of God. Godly leaders pray for God's kingdom to come and God's will to be done on earth as it is in heaven.

It is helpful for a servant of Christ to keep the end in view. There are some challenges that you face in leadership that can only be navigated with a "true north" star. Joan of Arc, at her trial, testified to the critical importance of an eternal perspective.

> Every man gives his life for what he believes. Every woman gives her life for what she believes. Sometimes people believe in little or nothing yet they give their lives to that little or

nothing. One life is all we have and we live it as we believe in living it. And then it is gone. But to sacrifice what you are and live without belief, that's more terrible than dying. But there is a worse fate than dying, even of dying young. That is to commit yourself to something that at the end of life, at the portals of eternity, turns out to have betrayed you.

A Christian leader begins with the end in mind, God's grand plan, then works backward to find his place in the world.

What's going on in my current circle of influence?

LEADERS use what they discover in the bigger and much-bigger pictures to inform their current circle of influence. Out of their reservoir of knowledge about the world as it is, and the world as it should be, a leader figures out how to best make a difference. Leaders may not be able to change the world, but they can change *their* world.

Leaders tend to emerge in a context where leadership is required: a group that needs direction, or a situation that needs catalyzing. The greater the challenges, the more pressure and risk, the greater is the need for a dynamic leader. Sharon Smith, CEO of Girl Scouts, describes her emergence as a leader:

I think there was no single turning point for me in becoming a leader but a gradual recognition that I could have an influence on the direction of an organization or a project if I stepped forward and took responsibility. Often in these situations there was an absence of someone clearly taking the lead (even if there was a designated "leader") or willingness to say "I will" from others. In these instances, colleagues welcomed my stepping forward. I think that I have learned that people are hungry for leadership, especially when they feel committed to getting something done or are concerned about the welfare of the project or organization.

A leader's circle of influence may be formal (an organization) or informal (friends and associates). If he is part of an organization the leader will requisition the organization to achieve results. An organization, after all, is just a collection of choices looking for decisions, problems looking for solutions and questions looking for answers. A leader steps up to provide impetus for an organization to fulfill its potential. If a leader is not part of an organization, he will exert informal influence on friends and associates to get something done.

What's going on with me?

IN addition to understanding what is going on around them, leaders have insight into what's going on inside them. They understand themselves. Before they step into a gap, they size themselves up for fit. They take stock to know how God can use them by asking several questions:

Who am I?

When Samuel was looking for a king to replace Saul in ancient Israel, he came to Jesse's oldest son, Eliab. Eliab was tall and handsome. He looked the part of a leader, much as Saul had years before. Surely this is the Lord's anointed, Samuel thought. But the Lord was quick to intervene: "Do not consider his appearance or his height, for I have rejected him. The Lord does not look at the things man looks at. Man looks at the outward appearance, but the Lord looks at the heart." A leader, likewise, studies his heart for readiness.

When professional coaches are deciding whether to draft a star collegiate player, they haul out their clipboards, tape measures, and stopwatches and put a number to everything. But **it's not just about the numbers. There are hidden qualities that differentiate a star player**.

Intangibles separate people into two categories: Those who have "it" and those who don't have "it." What is "it"? It may overlap what the Proverbs refer to as wisdom. The fear of the Lord is the beginning of "it." Fools don't have "it." "It" brings prosperity and a good life. Whatever its makeup, it begins with the prefix self-. People with "it" have mastered the uniquely human ability to "get outside themselves" and look back. They self-correct based on what they see.

The emerging science of emotional intelligence (EQ) may have stumbled onto "it." EQ (as defined by Daniel Goleman in Primal Leadership) has identified four intelligence domains and associated competencies, two of which begin with "self-":

Self-Awareness

- Emotional self-awareness: Reading one's own emotions and recognizing their impact; using "gut sense" to guide decisions

- Accurate self-assessment: Knowing one's strengths and limits

- Self-confidence: A sound sense of one's own self-worth and capabilities

Self-Management

- Emotional self-control: Keeping disruptive emotions and impulses under control

- Transparency: Displaying honesty and integrity; trustworthiness

- Adaptability: Flexibility in adapting to changing situations or overcoming obstacles

- Achievement: The drive to improve performance to meet inner standards of excellence

- Initiative: Readiness to act and seize opportunities

- Optimism: Seeing the upside in events

The study of emotional intelligence has highlighted the primacy of personal mastery. Simply put, **before you can effectively manage others, you must learn to manage yourself**. The toughest management challenge is always oneself.

People who stay on the path of self-development for years may achieve what John Maxwell calls "personhood," a level where people follow you because of who you are and what you represent. According to Daniel Goleman's research, the two sides to this highest form of leadership are Professional Will and Personal Humility:

Professional Will

Creates superb results; is a clear catalyst toward change.

Demonstrates an unwavering resolve to do whatever must be done to produce the best long-term results, no matter how difficult.

Sets the standard of building an enduring
great story; will settle for nothing less.

Looks in the mirror, not out the window, to apportion
responsibility for poor results, never blaming
other people, external factors, or bad luck.

Personal Humility

Demonstrates a compelling modesty, shunning
public adoration; never boastful.

Acts with quiet, calm determination; relies principally on
inspired standards, not inspiring charisma, to motivate.

Channels ambition into the ministry, not the self; sets up
successors for even greater success in the next generation.

Looks out the window, not in the mirror, to
apportion credit for the success of the enterprise – to
the Lord, other people, and external factors.

The cultivated self is a leader's greatest asset. The first Army leadership manual coined the phrase, "Be, Know, Do." The sequence is instructive. We are first and foremost human beings, not human doings. Good leadership requires a well-rounded, well-balanced person. As Bill Hybels says, "The best gift you can give the people you lead is a healthy, energized, fully surrendered, focused self." Unresolved character defects have derailed many promising leaders. A leader must be comfortable in his own skin, able to own both strengths and inadequacies. Leaders must lead from a healthy core.

Personal growth continues long after a person steps into a leadership position. A leader must be willing to grow along with the organization, as Edwin Markham penned,

We are blind until we see

That in the human plan

Nothing is worth the making

If it does not make the man.

Why build these cities glorious

If man unbuilded goes?

In vain we build the world

Unless the builder also grows.

Personal growth is so critical because it gets at the essence of what attracts followers. When people follow a leader, they don't follow a skill set, a technique or a message. **People follow a person. They may appreciate a skill, or a technique or a message, but people ultimately follow a person.**

A leader's integrity, or lack thereof, may not be initially revealed (talent can sometimes mask character defects), but over time a leader's integrity becomes the focus for followers. Truth and time walk hand in hand together. Integrity is "an unimpaired or unmarred condition, soundness, utter sincerity, candor, avoidance of deception, lack of artificiality, being complete and undivided." Integrity is closely related to the word "integer" - a "whole" number (no fractions, or percentages). In baking, we say that bread has integrity when all the parts touch, when it is of equal consistency. Integrity is the difference between bread and the ingredients that make up bread. Integrity means we have not compartmentalized our lives. To the extent that there is inconsistency, we lack integrity. We lack integrity when we lack consistency between our ideals and our behaviors. For instance:

When we say that we love our brother, but will not
go out of our way to help him, we lack integrity.

When we say that Jesus is Lord, but do not do
what he tells us to do, we lack integrity.

When we say that we are committed to ministry, but then
do not get involved in ministering, we lack integrity.

When we say that we believe in Christian liberty, but do
not give others freedom to be different, we lack integrity.

When we say that we are Christ's servants, but then
we will not reach out to others, we lack integrity.

When we say that we have the Holy Spirit, but do not
evidence the fruit of the spirit, we lack integrity.

When we say that we are committed to unity, but
then spread gossip and strife, we lack integrity.

When we say that we are Christian, but do not
respond like Christ, we lack integrity.

Integrity is "wholiness" - the unity of our ideals and practice. When Jesus was asked to pick the greatest of all the commandments, he stated, "Love the Lord your God with all your heart and with all your soul and with all your mind. This is the first and greatest commandment." The key word and the formidable challenge to spiritual integrity is found in the word "all," captured so elegantly in this prayer of Joe Bayly:

Lord of reality, make me real.....not plastic, synthetic,
pretend, phony......an actor playing out his part, hypocrite.

I don't want to keep a prayer list, but to pray, nor agonize
to find your will, but to obey what I already know.

I don't want to argue theories of inspiration,
but submit to Your Word.

I don't want to explain the difference between
eros and philos and agape, but to love.

I don't want to sing as if I mean it - I want to mean it.

I don't want to tell it like it is, but to be it like you want it.

I don't want to think another needs me, but
I need him - else I'm not complete.

I don't want to tell others how to do it, but
to do it; I don't want to have to be always
right, but to admit it when I'm wrong.

I don't want to be a census taker, but an obstetrician,
nor an involved person, a professional, but a friend.

I don't want to be insensitive, but to hurt where
other people hurt, nor to say "I know how you feel,"
but to say "God knows" and I'll try...if you'll be
patient with me, and meanwhile I'll be quiet.

I don't want to scorn the cliches of others, but
to mean everything I say...including this.

What do I believe?

To be a leader you have to know what you believe. You have to be a person of faith, philosophy, ideas. You have to know what is important to you. If you don't know, then you are not leading, you are following. Leaders have clear ideas and values, based on knowledge and experience. When studies are done about admired historical leaders, at the top of the list are Abraham Lincoln and Martin Luther King, Jr. Others who make the list are Winston Churchhill, Mother Theresa and

FDR. What is the consistent theme of this list? They were all people with strong beliefs about matters of principle. They had cultivated a vital spiritual core. As Dan Rather said about Nelson Mandela, "You know where he stands....you know what he believes....you know what he's willing to die for — and there's tremendous power in that!"

A leader is called to be a beacon of conviction in a sea of relativism - a rock of Gibraltar against the swirling winds of capitulation. While others are willing to sell their birthright for a bowl of pottage, the leader navigates by principle rather than politics. Thomas Jefferson's advice was "In matters of style, swim with the current, in matters of principle, stand like a rock."

Conviction is the difference between good ideas and governing ideas.

Good Idea	Governing Idea
Will commit to...	Will sacrifice for...
Will contemplate the cost of...	No cost is too great...
Negotiable...	Non-negotiable...
Ask others to subscribe...	Demand others to subscribe...
Decided by the group...	Decided by the individual...
For a season...	For a lifetime...
Can be changed...	Cannot be changed...
External compliance acceptable...	Internal ownership essential...
Can be political...	Never political...

Leaders resist the temptation to accommodate themselves to the world in order to influence it. A leader knows if he compromises he will not be working from a point of strength, but of weakness. As Jesus said, the finest lights shine brightly; the choicest salt possesses distinct taste. There is tremendous power in conviction. Others may not like what a leader stands for, but at least they'll know he stands.

Stephen Covey, in his book *Seven Habits of Highly Effective People*, chronicles the tectonic shift in American culture in the past 100 years from a "character ethic" to a "personality ethic." Businesses have moved resources from research and development to marketing and public relations. Politicians have become more concerned with sound bites and slogans than policies and platforms. This is the age of style over substance. As Howard Hendricks states, "The greatest crisis in the world is a crisis of leadership, and the greatest crisis in leadership is a crisis of character."

> Leadership development efforts aimed at spiritual leaders all too often have neglected these issues of the heart. With the now decades-long emphasis on ministry as mechanic (how to counsel parishioners, how to grow a church, how to prepare a sermon, how to raise money, and the how-to list goes on and on), attention to the core being of spiritual leaders has gotten squeezed out in favor of more glamorous pursuits, or at least pursuits that make the minister and his ministry "successful."….However, all the leadership insight and expertise on the planet cannot, in the end, overcome a case of spiritual heart disease or "heart failure." …Functionalism has replaced spiritual formation. Program manipulation and methodological prowess often serve as mere stop gaps to substitute for genuine spiritual leadership.
>
> - Reggie McNeal, *A Work of Heart*

Ronald Reagan was an admired American president in large part because he knew what he believed. He believed that communism was evil, that it takes away people's freedom. He believed that government had to reduce in size. Interestingly, these weren't necessarily popular ideas when he developed them, in the 1950s and 1960s. Barry Goldwater lost his bid for President of the United State with these ideas. But Reagan wasn't taking polls. This is what he really believed. So when he was elected, he didn't have to be anything different than he was. He could lead in alignment with his beliefs, and do so with integrity. So impacting was his leadership that he changed the map of Europe.

What do I care about?

CARING is central to leadership. **Leaders care about others, about the situation, and about making a difference.** Leadership involves thinking, to be sure, but also feeling. To be a leader is to be dissatisfied — always joyful, but never satisfied. There is an appropriate discontent that brews in the heart of a leader. Leaders care too much to allow things to remain as they are. Something must be done.

When leaders start looking around, eventually something grabs them that won't let them go. I'm not so sure that a leader catches a vision, as much as a vision catches them. They can't keep from being enamored with what needs to be done. Their passion finds a purpose.

Leaders are ambitious. Ambition may be called by many names: motivation, drive, enthusiasm, or achievement. Regardless of how it is described, **a certain amount of drive is essential to leadership.** It is estimated that only 2% of adults have any sense of urgency. It is out of this tiny population that the greatest leaders will emerge. Many leaders have what psychologists have identified as "need-achievement" – the desire to do well for the sake of an inner feeling of personal accomplishment.

Christian leaders may be just as ambitious as non-Christian leaders. Christian leadership is only distinctive in its motivations - the "why" of its drive. Love has to be the driving force for a Christian leader. As Max DePree writes in *Leading Without Power,* "We are working primarily for love." John Stanford, a successful leader in the military and education, has often been asked the secret of his success. He says, "When anyone asks me that question, I tell them I have the secret to success in life. The secret of success is to stay in love. Staying in love gives you the fire to ignite other people, to see inside other people, to have a greater desire to get things done than other people. A person who is not in love doesn't really feel the kind of excitement that helps them to get ahead and to lead others and to achieve. I don't know any other fire, any other thing in life that is more exhilarating and is more positive a feeling than love is."

One of the most successful executives of one of the largest corporations in America was asked about how he achieved such stunning results. He said, "I just took principles from the Bible and put them into action on the job." He added, "Love is a legitimate business strategy."

> If I speak in the tongues of men and of angels, but have not
> love, I am only a resounding gong or a clanging cymbal.
> If I have the gift of prophecy and can fathom all mysteries
> and all knowledge, and if I have a faith that can move
> mountains, but have not love, I am nothing. If I give all I

possess to the poor and surrender my body to the flames, but
have not love, I gain nothing.   - 1 Corinthians 13:1-3

In God's scheme of things, **love is more important than giftedness,
insight or accomplishments**. Let me paraphrase 1 Corinthians 13:1-
3, and make it personal, like this....

If, as a pastor, I can attract an audience which fills all of the
bleachers in the largest stadium, or if I address millions on
television, or if I sit back quietly in a book-lined study and
write book after book which lands on the best seller list, and
if I am not a loving person, I am only a successful huckster
displaying his wares. If I finish my doctorate degree and
hang the diploma proudly in my office, or if I lead a massive
charge to change the moral fabric of our community, and if
my church becomes the fastest growing church in America,
and I don't have love, I am only a paper moon shining
over a cardboard sea. And if I triple my tithe and send
mission teams around the world, and if I break my health
in ministry and outreach, and if I don't have love, I have
only wasted my time and shouted vainly into the wind.

Love is the distinctive quality of followers of Jesus Christ. Jesus
said, "By this all men will know that you are my disciples, if you love
one another."

What is love? Love is a commitment to the other person's well-
being. Love is what seeks the best for its object. It is not so much a
feeling to be felt as an action to be learned. The Apostle Paul said,
"Love is patient, love is kind. It does not envy, it does not boast, it is
not proud. It is not rude, it is not self-seeking, it is not easily angered,

16

it keeps no record of wrongs. Love does not delight in evil but rejoices with the truth. It always protects, always trusts, always hopes, always perseveres. Love never fails."

The scripture informs us that we can love others, no matter how they may relate to us. There are times when people seem to be below us. At these times love is patient and kind. There are times when people seem to be above us. At these times love does not envy. There are times when people seem to be behind us. At these times, love does not boast, it is not proud, it is not rude. No matter where people are in relationship to us, there's a way for a leader to love them.

How courageous am I?

LEADERS are courageous. They possess emotional fortitude and psychological hardiness. Most people think if you are afraid, you don't have courage. Courage is the management of fear, not the absence of it. It is getting your butterflies to fly in formation. It is going forward in spite of doubt and fear.

Especially in turbulent times, leaders must behave like emotional and intellectual anchors. They must have the courage of their convictions. They must be willing to take principled action when others make excuses or quit. They must be able to endure feelings and learn from them, instead of immediately reacting to them.

> Leaders who go the distance have a heavy-duty resilience.
> Somebody is always trying to pull you down when you're
> a leader. And you cannot be vacillating back and forth
> with the wind. There can be a wind when you're successful
> and everyone agrees with you. Or there can be a wind

when you're not successful and everyone disagrees with
you. Courage gives a leader the ability to stand straight
and not sway no matter which way the wind blows.

- Mike Krzyzewski, *Leading With The Heart*

A man who escaped prison was asked how he got over the wall.
"It's easy. Getting over the wall isn't really that hard when you've lost
your fear of death. It's never really the wall that holds you. It's the fear
of dying." He realized it was not an external barrier that was holding
him back; it was an internal barrier. Fear is often the real barrier.

Courage is almost a contradiction in terms. It means a strong
desire to live taking the form of a readiness to die. "He that
will lose his life, will save it," is not a piece of mysticism for
saints and heroes. It is a piece of everyday advice for sailors
or mountaineers. It might be printed in an Alpine guide or
a drill book. This paradox is the whole principle of courage;
even of quite earthly or quite brutal courage. A man cut off
by the sea may save his life if he will risk it on the precipice.
He can only get away from death by continually stepping
within an inch of it. A soldier surrounded by enemies, if
he is to cut his way out, needs to combine a strong desire
for living with a strange carelessness about dying. He must
not merely cling to life, for then he will be a coward, and
will not escape. He must not merely wait for death, for
then he will be a suicide, and will not escape. He must
seek his life in a spirit of furious indifference to it; he must
desire life like water and yet drink death like wine. No
philosopher, I fancy, has ever expressed this romantic riddle
with adequate lucidity, and I certainly have not done so.

But Christianity has done more: it has marked the limits of courage, showing the distance between him who dies for the sake of living and him who dies for the sake of dying.

- G.K. Chesterton

Firefighters, obviously, must exhibit courage. They must regularly manage their fears. Yet an incredible transformation takes place as soon as they go inside the building. They literally step into the fear, and because they do, the fear disappears. They are one hundred percent in the present moment. They are then able to concentrate on fighting the fire, evacuating the people and doing all the things they are trained to do. By confronting their fear, they can focus on the immediate situation and get the job done. That's leadership.

They Envision A Preferable Future

LEADERS not only define current reality, they look into the future and see something better. They behave more like thermostats than thermometers. They set the temperature, instead of just reading it. Where there are obstacles, they see opportunity.

Often, to envision a preferable future, a leader looks farther into the future than others are willing or able to do. Marcus Buckingham, in *The One Thing You Need To Know,* says that "What defines a leader is his preoccupation with the future. Leaders are fascinated with the future. You are never satisfied with the present, because in your head you can see a better future."

They See Opportunities.

LEADERS find opportunities where others do not. And if opportunities are not apparent, a leader feels it's his job to create them. While managers look inward, leaders are constantly searching outward for alternative routes forward. Leaders are visionaries. They have a clear mental image of a preferable future, as Andrea Cunningham describes:

> There is definitely something special about a leader. He
> or she seems to have the ability to mold the future with
> nothing more than an idea. It's an idea that is so strong,
> it won't die - not with criticism, lack of support or
> funding, not even with failure. This is called VISION.

I can't say exactly where vision comes from, but once it's born in a leader, that person is miraculously endowed with certain qualities that protect the vision and enable its achievement. There may be a vision lurking inside you if you have these qualities:

- Confidence…An undying and unquestionable belief in your abilities.

- Discipline…The stick-to-it-iveness to do whatever it takes to make things happen.

- Energy…The electricity to light up the organization and keep it running.

- Motivation…The desire to make heroes out of your subordinates.

- Inspiration…The personality to get people to join your parade.

It was Walt Disney's vision that led to the creation of Disneyland in

California, and Disneyworld in Florida. Unfortunately, he didn't live to walk down the Main Street of his new Magic Kingdom in Florida or to stroll from pavilion to pavilion in Epcot Center. He died in 1965, almost five years before Walt Disney World opened. On the day the Florida park opened, someone commented to Mike Vance, creative director of Walt Disney Studios, "Isn't it too bad Walt Disney didn't live to see this?" "He did see it," Vance replied simply. "That why it's here."

A vision is like a fingerprint; there are no two exactly alike. Vision creates direction, distinctiveness and excitement. **Vision becomes a bold reason for living. It is a badge of purpose that can be worn with conviction.**

A leader has to see farther ahead than those he leads. A boss has to see a bigger picture than his crew. The higher your vantage point the farther you get to see and the farther you have to see. A person on the front lines can afford to have a limited perspective. Not so for the commander in chief. While others are looking to the end of the block, the leader is seeing around the corner.

They Take Responsibility for Results.

LEADERS not only envision a preferable future, they take responsibility for bringing it about. Leadership is the assumption of accountability. Leaders "own the project." As Andrea Cunningham states, "Leadership isn't about popularity and it isn't always fun. It's about owning the responsibility to make a difference in the world and signing up people to make it happen."

The power to act is never released until a decision has been made.

Once a leader is committed, things start happening.

> Until one is committed, there is hesitance, the chance
> to draw back, and always ineffectiveness....The moment
> one definitely commits oneself...a whole stream of events
> issue from the decision, raising in one's favor all manner
> of unforeseen incidents and material assistance which
> no man could have dreamed would come his way.
>
> - Johann Wolfgang von Goethe

Leadership stems from personal decisions that release energy into the organization. Once a leader has decided, energy can be fully devoted to accomplishment of the objective. Until then, energy is diffused. As the Bible says, "A double-minded man is unstable in all his ways."

Leaders are willing to pay the price for the accomplishment of the dream. This means that leaders have to be buyers primarily, not sellers. They have the greatest buy-in. They make the greatest personal commitment. They invest themselves, knowing full well that the payment will be ongoing.

All leaders possess the gift of faith. They have a willingness to stretch themselves and go after goals that others think are too far out there, or impossible to accomplish. They say to themselves, "This needs doing, and by God's grace, I'm going for it." They offer analysis, certainly, but also action. Leaders see and then seize opportunities.

Leaders Do What
Needs to Be Done

LEADERS not only see what needs to be done, they do what needs to be done. They are action oriented, with a focused drive. Leaders need to see not just activity, but results.

Dwight Eisenhower once said, "Leadership is action, not position." There are three kinds of people in the world - those who don't know what's happening, those who watch what's happening, and those who make things happen. Leaders are among the third group.

> (A leader is one) who guides activities of others and who
> himself acts and performs to bring those activities about. He
> is capable of performing acts which will guide a group in
> achieving objectives. He takes the capacities of vision and
> faith, has the ability to be concerned and to comprehend,
> exercises action through effective and personal influence
> in the direction of an enterprise and the development of
> the potential into the practical and/or profitable means.
>
> - Ted Engstrom

When God creates a leader, he gives him the capacity to make things happen. **What does a leader do? Whatever needs to be done.** Leaders mobilize the appropriate resources to improve the situation.

An effective leader begins as a prophet, but then quickly graduates to practitioner. Or as Roger von Oech describes, a leader has to wear more than one hat: an explorer hat (to find the idea), an artist hat (to be creative with the idea), a judge hat (to be creative and critical of the idea), and a warrior hat (to take the idea into battle).

It's one thing to know what needs to be done. It's another to understand how to make that happen. A leader is a catalyst for change. Change isn't change unless something changes. Leaders stage revolutions. They engage in disruption. They cause reactions. They churn the environment. They champion renewal. As the authors of *The Leadership Challenge* point out, "Leaders must challenge the process precisely because any system will unconsciously conspire to maintain the status quo and prevent change."

Surveys show that most people excel at either being dreamers or doers, but not both. Some preoccupy themselves with dreaming grand dreams, but have little follow-through or implementation. Others preoccupy themselves with activity with little vision of the bigger picture. For effectiveness, the leader must have both a worthy destination, and the ability to get there with others.

They Enlist Others

ONCE a leader has clarity of vision, he sets out to enlist others for the expedition. A leader realizes that while it may all start with him, it doesn't all depend on him. A leader sees a better future, then helps others see what he sees. If a person cannot envision a better future, he is not a leader. If he can't rally people to see what he sees, he is not a leader, either.

A leader is a person who rallies others to a better future.

- Marcus Buckingham

A leader is someone you will follow to a place you wouldn't go by yourself.

- Joel Barker

Leadership is the ability to obtain followers.

- James Georges

Leadership is all about influencing people. As John Maxwell defines it, "Leadership is influence." You may not consider yourself a leader, but if others are being influenced by you, you are, in fact, a leader. On the other hand, you may consider yourself a leader, but if no one is being influenced by you, then you are not leading. A popular leadership proverb says, "He who thinks he is leading, but looks over his shoulder and sees no one is following, is only taking a walk."

Leadership is something which is inferred by followers. Peter Drucker opines: "There is only one characteristic common to all leaders: Followers."

People respond to a worthy vision passionately presented by a gifted leader. They do not respond when either the cause or the leadership are deemed inadequate. Most great leaders don't try to be great leaders. They try to make things better for people. Leaders continually think "other people." Leaders want to help other people win. **They die to the dream of being a success, and live to the dream of being a**

blessing.

One-time Vice Presidential candidate Admiral James Stockdale declared, "Leadership must be based on good will….It means obvious and wholehearted commitment to helping followers…What we need for leaders are men of heart who are so helpful that they, in effect, do away with the need of their jobs. But leaders like that are never out of a job, never out of followers. Strange as it sounds, great leaders gain authority by giving it away."

Formally designated hierarchy is not required for leadership to emerge. In the best cases, leaders are identified officially only after they are established unofficially. When a leader cares about people and their success, in response they wish him well, and want him to succeed. They want to go along with him, because they get along with him. His credibility is gained through personal ability and performance, rather than formal positional power.

Leadership depends on personal relationships. Prior to assuming leadership your job is "me." Subsequent to assuming leadership your job is "us." As John Maxwell says, "**A successful person is evaluated by personal progress. A successful leader is evaluated by group progress**." A leader believes in delivery of the dream with a team. He knows how to get others to link their lives with his to accomplish something great. He can get the support of others.

Noel Tichy, in *The Leadership Engine*, defines leadership as "the capacity to get things done through others by changing people's mindsets and energizing them to action." A leader's first and most essential task is to create a coalition. A great leader finds a balance between the ends (getting results) and the means (how he gets them). A driven person could possibly get the job done more expeditiously by himself. But leadership is about creating a way for other people to contribute to making something extraordinary happen. Understanding the destination takes IQ; taking others with you takes EQ.

They Share.

LEADERS find a way to make people confident in and excited by what comes next. If you are a visionary, you know what you want. A mature visionary can express what they want to see with sufficient conviction to win people over. One way or another, leaders prompt others to conclude, "This is a compelling mission. I'm in!"

Leaders begin to engage others by creating dissatisfaction with the status quo. They stir the pot. A leader is a change agent - the chief disorganizational officer. A leader stems the tide of complacency.

A leader then appeals to people's values, interests, hopes and dreams. Stephen Covey says, "Leadership is communicating value so clearly that people come to see it in themselves." Kouzes and Pousner say, "No matter how grand the dream of an individual visionary, if others don't see in it the possibility of realizing their own hopes and desires, they won't follow."

Leaders, by definition, are people who change things (minds, circumstances, outcomes, etc.). **Leaders create the right kind of tension, a tension that causes people to step up to another level of commitment or involvement**. They cultivate hunger for which they can provide the right kind of food. As John Ortberg states, "The production and management of discomfort is one of the great pastoral arts." Leadership is the management of meaning.

A leader's job is to change people's perspective on a situation.

Leaders achieve their effectiveness chiefly through the stories they relate. A leader believes that thoughts are causes and conditions are effects. A leader uses imagination and vivid description to bring everyone up to a new level of understanding the challenges and possibilities. He replaces an old story with a new story. In addition to telling stories, leaders embody the stories they tell.

Warren Bennis, in *The Leader As Storyteller,* says "Effective leaders put words to the formless longings and deeply felt needs of others. They create communities out of words." To be a leader, you have to be able to get your ideas into the minds of other people. **Leaders say it well, say it often, say it simply and say it passionately**. They are the programmers of society. One way or another, they get their message across. They distill the story line so that it can be easily grasped. They infect social networks with their ideas. They make the vision compelling and relevant.

In 1934 Walt Disney had a vision for a full-length animated feature film called *Snow White and the Seven Dwarfs*. So clear was his vision that he invited 300 artists to join him in an empty sound stage, where he acted out the story. Sitting on folding chairs, the audience watched Disney as he personally acted out the parts of Snow White and each of the dwarfs, and took the writers through the story scene by scene. The finished product contained 250,000 individual drawings, and throughout production the artists harkened back to the hours-long enactment of Mr. Disney as their guiding light. When the movie debuted on December 21, 1937 it blew away every box-office record, bringing in over $8 million its first year. Disney captured the imagination of the viewing public, but first he captured the imagination of 300 artists who made it happen.

Leaders do not manage reality, they shape reality. A leader
charts an unhesitating, unequivocal course toward progress.
The foundation of effective leadership is thinking through
the organization's mission, defining it and establishing
it, clearly and visibly. The leader sets the goals, sets the
priorities, and sets and maintains the standards.

- Peter Drucker

People are waiting for a cause that is worthy of their lives. When
Jesus called his first followers (Peter, Andrew, James, John) to follow
him, he asked them to join him in a mission to change the world. He
used vivid word pictures to get his ideas across. Ideation sets apart
great leaders. Initially, a leader picks ideas. Then he picks people to
carry out these ideas. Then he mobilizes those leaders to move out in
pursuit of the goal.

The job of a good leader is to articulate a vision that
others are inspired to follow. The definition of good
leadership always comes back to what the leader says
we stand for and how that leader makes everybody in
an organization understand how to make that vision
active. A lot of people write mission statements, but
their words don't come off the page. Leadership is about
making a vision happen – what I call "vision acts." If
you say you're about something, then what activities in
your company indicate the reality behind these words?

- Lorraine Monroe

Setting the mission is a defining moment for a leader. A man
who knows where he is going will accomplish so much more than the

person without clearly defined goals. A wise leader aligns people to the mission, rather than to a personality or methodology. A leader lets people know exactly what he wants them to do. The place of agreement is the place of power.

They Inspire.

NAPOLEON said, "A leader is a dealer in hope." Followers want to see the best and bravest from their leaders. Good leaders don't say, "Things are bad, they are not going to get better, follow me." Leaders convey promise. They are optimistic. They bring people solutions. They build confidence. They demonstrate conviction. Winston Churchill, who was a dealer in hope, once said, "The pessimist sees difficulty in every opportunity. The optimist sees opportunity in every difficulty."

After the September 11th, 2001 attacks on the World Trade Center buildings in New York City, then-mayor Rudolph Guiliani demonstrated hope-filled leadership, when he said: "The people in New York City will be whole again. We are going to come out of this emotionally stronger, politically stronger, much closer together as a city, and we're going to come out of this economically stronger, too." What did he do? He focused on the future and what could be done. You cannot be a leader without being hopeful. You certainly cannot be a Christian leader without being hopeful. The pace of the leader becomes the pace of the team.

There is a learned optimism that accompanies leadership. You can see confidence in a leader's face, in his demeanor, in his swagger. A leader shows his team the face they need to see. A leader's job is to drive out fear. Rick Warren suggests, "Most people probably know how bad they are, but they need to hear how good they can become." As a

Christian leader, the gospel gives us a bias that something redemptive can happen. In a study of American elections, researchers found that voters were influenced by language that was "highly certain, highly optimistic, highly realistic, and highly active."

> The fundamental task of leaders is to prime good feelings
> in those they lead....Great leaders move us. They ignite
> our passion and inspire the best in us. When we try to
> explain why they are so effective, we speak of strategy,
> vision, or powerful ideas. But the reality is much more
> primal: Great leadership works through the emotions....
> **the leader acts as the group's emotional guide**.
>
> - Daniel Goleman, *Primal Leadership*

At the end of the movie *Apollo 13*, the lives of three astronauts hang in the balance in a spaceship far from earth. They depend on a community of engineers in Houston, charged with saving their lives. One of the engineers expresses his dismay that this will be the worst catastrophe in NASA history. The character played by Ed Harris straightens up, squares his shoulders and says, "To the contrary – with all due respect – I believe this will be our finest hour."

> The English word "coach" is derived from Kocs, the name
> of a village in northeastern Hungary, where carriages
> and carts were traditionally made. Nineteenth-century
> university students adopted the word as slang for "tutor."
> Instructors, it seems, took such an intense, personal interest
> in their students' progress that students felt conveyed
> through the exam as if driven in the instructor's carriage.
> We think the word, today, still conveys some of that
> spirit of close partnership and mutual responsibility.
>
> - Peter Senge, *The Dance of Change*

They Empower.

LEADERS help others to achieve what they could not achieve on their own. Leaders pave the way for others to have a smooth path to their dreams. The function of leadership is to produce more leaders, not more followers.

Developing the next generation of leaders is the greatest amplifier of a leader's impact. But becoming a leader who develops leaders instead of a leader who develops followers requires an entirely different focus. Consider some of the differences John Maxwell points out in his book *The 21 Irrefutable Laws of Leadership:*

Leaders who develop followers	**Leaders who develop leaders**
Need to be needed	Want to be succeeded
Focus on weaknesses	Focus on strengths
Develop the bottom 20 percent	Develop the top 20 percent
Treat people the same for fairness	Treat people as individuals for impact
Hoard power	Give power away
Spend time with others	Invest time in others
Grow by addition	Grow by multiplication
Impact only people they touch	Impact people beyond their reach

John Schnatter, founder of Papa John's Pizza, says, "It's my job to build the people who are going to build the company." I like that point of view. It is not his job to build the company. It is his job to build the people so that they can build the company. John Maxwell describes this principle as The Law of Legacy:

> Achievement comes to someone when he is able to do
> great things for himself. Success comes when he empowers
> followers to do great things with him. Significance comes
> when he develops leaders to do great things for him. But a
> legacy is created only when a person puts his organization
> into the position to do great things without him.

The role of leadership is not to drive people to change, as much as it is to create an environment that inspires, supports and leverages the latent imagination and initiative that exists within people. **Leaders create a climate in which the ideas and initiative of others can flourish**. Jack Welch believes, "The idea flow from the human spirit is unlimited. All you have to do is tap into the flow."

At Christ the King Community Church we have made empowerment one of our stated values. In our job descriptions we say "It is the role of paid staff to create and sustain an environment in which the people of CTK can execute their ministry with minimum obstacles and maximum fulfillment." Creating a climate that gets everyone's mind into the game is a huge part of what leadership is all about. Gene Bedley contrasts climate creators from climate destroyers:

Climate Creators	**Climate Destroyers**
Listeners	Talk incessantly
Facilitate discovery	Solely lecture
Transcend reality	Fix reality
Transmit information creatively	Transmit information mechanically
Stimulate active participation	Promote passive participation
Emphasize responsibility	Emphasize obedience
Foster creativity	Lock step systems
Engender continuous progress	Utilize arbitrary measures of achievement
Learning is teaching	Teaching is learning
Utilize others as peer resources	Perceive themselves as the only resource
Encouraging	Punitive
Build cooperation with competition	Utilize competition, neglect cooperation
Focus on others	Focus on themselves

A key talent of outstanding leaders is the ability to be led. As Irwin Federman says, "Leaders listen, take advice, lose arguments, and follow." Ben Franklin said, "He who cannot obey, cannot command." Leaders have to possess vision, but they also have to possess an ability to make course corrections as they go along.

Effective leaders take everyone's best ideas and incorporate them as possible. This is often difficult for leaders. After all, a leader may have achieved a position of leadership because he has known the right answers most of the time. But promotion eventually brings a leader to a place where the level of complexity and responsibility is unfamiliar. This new territory requires a leader to rely on the skills and competencies of others. No one is as smart as everyone.

> When leaders fail to empathize with, or to read the emotions of a group accurately, they create dissonance, sending needlessly upsetting messages. Dissonant leaders are the bosses people dread working for....When a leader is attuned to people's feelings and moves them in a positive direction, she/he exemplifies resonant leadership. When a leader triggers resonance, you can read it in people's eyes: They're engaged and they light up....A primal leadership dictum is that resonance amplifies and prolongs the emotional impact of leadership. The more resonant people are with each other, the less static are their interactions; resonance minimizes noise in the system ("more signal, less noise")....
> Emotional intelligence allows bad news, as well as good, to travel throughout the organization. "CEO disease" is the information vacuum around a leader created when people withhold important (and usually unpleasant) information. To become effective, leaders need to break through the information quarantine around them – and the conspiracy to keep them pleased, even if uninformed.
>
> - Daniel Goleman, *Primal Leadership*

Leaders sometimes get the insights they need from those above them (managers), sometimes from those around them (colleagues), and sometimes from those under them (subordinates). Studies show that most innovations come from ideas generated by followers. A leadership maxim is, "There's not much oxygen at the top of the mountain. The oxygen is down in the valley where the people live."

To gain the insights he needs, a leader develops what Peter Senge calls the ability to "balance advocacy with inquiry." This is the ability to hold a position, while at the same time holding it loosely, or seeing the other side. "The test of a first-rate mind," according to F. Scott Fitzgerald, "is the ability to hold two opposing ideas at the same time and still be able to function."

The humility required to "balance advocacy with inquiry" typically brings secondary benefits beside giving a leader better answers. It creates a better environment, with more team unity, trust and cohesion. **People love to be asked their opinion**. They feel valued when they are included. Inquiry also keeps the leader from becoming relationally isolated. As Chris Argyris says in *Overcoming Organizational Defenses*, "Loneliness at the top is a product of a reciprocal isolating dynamic of aloofness between subordinates and the executive."

The leader is first among equals. Daniel Boorstin, the Librarian for Congress, gives a lecture about amateurs and professionals. "The leader," he says, "is by definition an amateur — open to new vistas that training precludes from the professional." Leadership is a reciprocal relationship where listening ends up being as important as speaking.

They Follow Through

LEADERS get things done. Or better, they see to it that things get done. The measure of leadership is not the size of the chain of command. It is not receiving deference or honorary, positional titles. It is accomplishing something.

Leaders do what needs to be done, when it needs to be done, and I might add, whether they like doing it or not. As Albert Gray says, "The common denominator of **success lies in forming the habit of doing things that failures don't like to do.**"

> It is not the critic who counts, not the man who points out how the strong man stumbled, or where the doer of deeds could have done them better. The credit belongs to the man who is actually in the arena; whose face is marred by dust and sweat and blood; who strives valiantly; who errs and comes short again and again…who knows the great enthusiasms, the great devotions and spends himself in a worthy cause; who, at the worst, if he fails, at least fails while daring greatly, so that his place shall never be with those cold and timid souls who know neither victory nor defeat.
>
> - Teddy Roosevelt

They Execute.

LEADERS bring a project to completion by force of will. They know where they are going, how to get there, and how far they have to go to arrive.

Leaders have a bias toward action – toward activity. Because there is no better indicator of the health of a project than steady activity, leaders can appear impatient at times. As the old folk proverb goes: "The best time to plant a tree is 20 years ago. The second best time is now." A leader avoids talking about what "might" be, and instead talks about what "must" be. A leader's response to a good suggestion is, "Let's do it." Then it's on to the next decision. They know that a certain number of decisions they make may be wrong. But ultimately they play the odds and take action. As General Patton once said, "Give me a good plan executed with vigor right now, not a great plan executed next week."

Leaders understand that their personal competence creates credibility. Making a contribution to progress is an important complement to talking about progress. Leaders model the way through priority management and personal excellence. Their exemplary personal performance inspires others to follow suit.

> Leaders are men and women who have chosen the right
> profession. They're good at it, and because they're good at
> it, they like it, and because they like it, they're even better
> at it. They're so good at it that they'd rather work than
> play. They're naturals, and excelling comes naturally as well.
> They've understood their field from the start, and they've
> studied it without even knowing they've studied it.
>
> - David Halberstam,
> *The Leadership That Cannot Be Taught*

As a leader develops competence, he should develop another "c" - consistency. Willie Mays was right on when he said, "It's easy to go out and be good once in a while. The magic is to do it every day." A leader has to be consistent. Once a leader arrives at an acceptable level of competence, he must turn his attention to reinforcing that new level. Better to consistently deliver a 7 than to deliver a 9 one week, a 3 the next, and a 5 the next.

A leader must be consistent not just in performance, but personality. A leader is an important symbolic figure. When people see something significantly "different" about their leader, they tend to question all that they believe they know. Consistency is reassuring. Behavior can either bestow or withdraw legitimacy. The world is too unpredictable. Leaders should not be. Leadership credibility grows as a leader consistently adds value to others over time.

> When I work with executive teams, I explain that if the CEO's behavior is ninety-five percent healthy while the rest of the organization is just fifty percent sound, I'll choose to focus on that crucial and leveraged five percent that makes up the remainder of the CEO's behavior.
>
> - Patrick Lencioni, *Five Temptations of a CEO*

Consistency separates great leaders from average ones, and great organizations from average ones. Can people count on the leader to deliver? Is the impact predictable? By producing, he puts himself in an even stronger position as a leader, where others look to him for advice and direction.

Dallas Willard says a great danger is to invite others to live a life you yourself are not willing to live. When a leader requires more of others than he does himself, it sets up an unhealthy environment. A real leader must be the change he is looking for in the world. But a corollary to Willard's warning is that leaders do invite others to live a life that they themselves are living. Having first given attention to their personal performance, a leader now gives his attention to the group's performance.

A leader is a coach. If you want to be a leader you have to be prepared and you have to prepare others. Leaders engage in performance planning, day to day coaching and performance evaluation. They praise, redirect and reprimand. As things change for the better, a leader benchmarks the progress.

A leader makes certain that people have the skills and resources they need and spurs them to work up to capacity. Each enterprise has the same six resources with which to work: Money, Time, People, Information, Technology, Facilities. A leader allocates resources to fulfill the strategic objectives of the enterprise. There are also "thumbprint decisions" that a leader must make (e.g. key staff hires) that will have disproportionate impact on the enterprise's success or failure.

> A leader is responsible for everything that happens in his organization. If he notices a problem, he must become a problem- solver. He must act swiftly and decisively. A lot of people have good ideas, and good values, and they can even energize others. But for some reason they are not able to make the tough calls. That is what separates, for me, whether or not someone can lead a business.
>
> - Jack Welch

Leaders who excel at execution immerse themselves in a few critical details that "make all the difference." They constantly probe and question. They measure and reward the specific behavior they want. They bring weaknesses to light and rally their team to correct them. Dwight Eisenhower, for example, had an insatiable curiosity for details. In the war, he always asked about the weather report – not just what the forecast was, but how his people came up with the forecast. If he hadn't questioned the weather, the timing of the landing on Omaha Beach would have been misguided. You never know when small details will become the determining factor.

A lot of success that we think comes from natural talent really comes from preparation. Leaders prepare the organization for what's coming. Excellent leaders think through scenarios. They spend a disproportionate amount of time in preparation. By preparing for the anticipated, they are better able to respond to the unanticipated. Because they deliberate with caution, they are able to act with decision. Leaders walk the rim of the canyon so that they can tell their team when another set of rapids is coming.

They Persist.

LEADERS chart a path toward a desired future and continue on that path despite obstacles and resistance. They keep the challenge alive. They exercise conscious oversight of both the people and the process to stay on track.

Leaders hate regression. Leaders think continuous improvement. One of the easiest ways to spot a leader who is no longer leading is to see him become increasingly involved in outside boards and committees. The enterprise begins to suffer as he loses focus.

> The person who is a little less conceptual but is absolutely
> determined to succeed will usually find the right people
> to get them to achieve objectives. I'm not knocking

education or looking for dumb people. But if you have to choose between someone with a staggering IQ and an elite education who's gliding along, and someone with a lower IQ but who is absolutely determined to succeed, you'll always do better with the second person.

- Larry Bossidy, *Execution*

Winston Churchill once defined leadership as "going from failure to failure without losing enthusiasm." Dr. W. Edwards Deming called it "constancy of purpose."

Leaders stay fixed on the end in mind. Even when others waver, a leader remains dedicated. No matter how big the rock, he knows that if he just keeps pounding it is going to bust. In the end, the race is won by the right objectives being relentlessly pursued. A leader never forgets what's at stake, and never gives up.

Others' disbelief and fear only reinforce the leader's resolve, and prove that the adventure is thoroughly challenging and worthwhile. Persistence maintains a sense of hope, even in the face of difficulty. "Apprehension is impressive," Charles Swindoll states, "until determination pulls rank on it and forces it to salute."

There is always a test of a leader's resolve in implementing the strategy. Commitment on the part of a leader should be viewed as a process rather than a status. Jay Leno's advice to aspiring comedians is "Just stay on the road." We may have to renew our commitment to lead many times. It will surely be tested. But we can go a long way with the right heart and determination. In *Zen and The Art of Motorcycle Maintenance*, Robert Pirsig refers to this vigor as "gumption."

If you're going to repair a motorcycle, an adequate supply of gumption is the first and most important tool. If you haven't got that you might as well gather up all the other tools and put them away, because they won't do you any good. Gumption is the psychic gasoline that keeps the whole thing going. If you haven't got it, there's no way the motorcycle can possibly be fixed. But if you have got it and know how to keep it, there's absolutely no way in the whole world that motorcycle can keep from getting fixed. It's bound to happen. Therefore the thing that must be monitored at all times and preserved before anything else is gumption.

A Christian leader must maintain a sense of anticipation and expectation that God is greater than the challenges being faced. Psychologists Suzanne C. Kobasa and Salvatore R. Maddi studied individuals in business who, although in the midst of highly stressful situations, nevertheless experienced low degrees of illness. They discovered that people with psychological hardiness:

1. Believed that they had an influence on their environment and acted consistently with that belief.

2. Consistently considered how to change situations for advantage and never accepted events at face value.

3. Regarded change as part of the normal course of events.

4. Viewed change as a helpful path to positive development.

5. Were committed to learning and personal transformation.

Hardiness is simply meeting the demands of the situation with character and courage. Frankly, at times, leadership can be pretty tough. Intense schedules. Issues. Being understaffed. People problems. It can get pretty crazy sometimes. At those times, a leader hangs tough. He doesn't shrink from the challenge. He digs deep. He stands in there. "When the going gets tough, the tough get going."

Ray Davis, CEO of Umpqua Bank, says one of the reasons a leader must be unyielding is that "so many people are cynical....They've been conditioned by bad management to expect that new programs introduced with bold announcements will eventually peter out." Years after Davis had implemented significant changes through discipline and persistence, employees confessed to him that when he came in as CEO with big ideas, they thought the initiatives would wane within six weeks. But Davis stayed the course and was unrelenting, until his followers became believers themselves.

In the book of Hebrews one of the overarching stories is that of the children of Israel being spooked by the giants in the promised land, and backing down. Evidently, God does not have a lot of patience with "shrink backers."

> Who were they who heard and rebelled? Were they not
> all those Moses led out of Egypt? And with whom was he
> angry for forty years? Was it not with those who sinned,
> whose bodies fell in the desert? And to whom did God
> swear that they would never enter his rest if not to those
> who disobeyed? So we see that they were not able to enter,
> because of their unbelief. Therefore, since the promise of
> entering his rest still stands, let us be careful that none
> of you be found to have fallen short of it. For we also
> have had the gospel preached to us, just as they did; but
> the message they heard was of no value to them, because
> those who heard did not combine it with faith.
>
> - Hebrews 3:16 – 4:2

Honestly, it is difficult for a wimp to be a leader. Yes, it's tough. Yes, people can be difficult. Yes, you get tired. Yes, there is never enough money. Yes, it is hard work. But a leader "gets over it" – whatever it is. Like my son's Little League coach tells the boys, "If you get hurt, spit on it ("pthew") and keep going."

Being a leader may exact pain and sacrifice. It certainly will take a man out of his comfort zone. But consider this stirring statement by a young African pastor, found among his papers after he was martyred:

> I'm a part of the fellowship of the unashamed. The die
> has been cast. I have stepped over the line. The decision
> has been made. I'm a disciple of His and I won't look
> back, let up, slow down, back away, or be still.
>
> My past is redeemed. My present makes sense. My future is
> secure. I'm done and finished with low living, sight walking,
> small planning, smooth knees, colorless dreams, tamed
> visions, mundane talking, cheap living, and dwarfed goals.
>
> I no longer need preeminence, prosperity, position,
> promotions, plaudits, or popularity. I don't have to
> be right, or first, or tops, or recognized, or praised, or
> rewarded. I live by faith, lean on His presence, walk by
> patience, lift by prayer, and labor by Holy Spirit power.
>
> My face is set. My gait is fast. My goal is heaven. My
> road may be narrow, my way rough, my companions
> few, but my guide is reliable and my mission is clear.
>
> I will not be bought, compromised, detoured,
> lured away, turned back, deluded or delayed.

I will not flinch in the face of sacrifice or hesitate in
the presence of the adversary. I will not negotiate
at the table of the enemy, ponder at the pool of
popularity, or meander in the maze of mediocrity.

I won't give up, shut up, or let up until I have
stayed up, stored up, prayed up, paid up, and
preached up for the cause of Christ.

I am a disciple of Jesus. I must give until I drop,
preach until all know, and work until He comes.
And when He does come for His own, He'll have no
problems recognizing me. My colors will be clear!

Statements like this resonate with a leader. He is prepared to serve
to the point of personal sacrifice.

They Applaud.

THE journey of a leader takes him from vision-caster to permission-
giver, and ultimately, to cheerleader. A leader holds the group's goals
as a sacred trust and communicates progress along the way, helping the
group to recognize its own success.

Leaders are encouragers. They recognize and celebrate the
contributions of others. They "tend to sustain their belief in others,"
says Stephen Shields, "even when there are counterindications. Leaders
give up on others with extreme reluctance because at some level they
feel that they are giving up on their ability to get the very best out of
others by doing so."

In one sequence of the Peanuts comic strip, Linus has just written a comic strip of his own, and he wants Lucy's opinion. "Would you read this and tell me if you think it's funny?" In the next frame you see Lucy patting her foot, and a grin comes across her face. She looks at Linus and says, "Well, Linus, who wrote this?" With his chest heaved out and great big grin on his face, Linus says, "Lucy, I wrote that." In the next frame you see Lucy wadding up the paper, throwing it to the side, and saying, "Well, then I don't think it's very funny." In the final frame, you see Linus picking up his comic strip, throwing his blanket over his shoulder, looking at Lucy and saying, "Big sisters are the crabgrass in the lawn of life." We find that humorous, but if we thought about it, I'm sure that we can recall people in a leadership position who were the crabgrass in the lawn of life.

Leaders, if they're not careful, can find themselves being more pessimistic than optimistic; more discouraging than encouraging. Encouragement is vital. Encouragement is the gasoline that drives the engine. We can't go anywhere without it. Encouragement helps a person overcome when they feel overwhelmed. Encouragement is like a cool breeze on a hot summer day — it revives and refreshes.

A great leader, when things go well, doesn't take credit, but gives recognition; and when things go poorly takes responsibility, and doesn't assign blame. You can spot an extraordinary leader when extraordinary results exist but no individual is stepping forth to claim all the credit.

> A leader is best
>
> When people barely know that he exists.
>
> Of a good leader, who talks little,
>
> When his work is done, his aim fulfilled,
>
> They will say, "We did this ourselves."
>
> - Taoism

In the research of Jim Collins' *Good To Great*, those who worked in great organizations continually used words like quiet, humble, modest, reserved, shy, gracious, mild-mannered, self-effacing, and understated to describe their leaders. Winston Churchill exemplified these qualities. During his eightieth birthday party, he addressed his role in Great Britain's history:

> I have never accepted what many people have kindly
> said – namely that I inspired the nation.   Their will was
> resolute and remorseless, and as it proved, unconquerable.
> It fell to me to express it. It was the nation and the race
> dwelling all round the globe that had the lion's heart. I
> had the luck to be called upon to give the roar.

Many will wonder how a great leader can possess both extraordinary influence and humility. It cannot be any other way.

> The leaders who work most effectively, it seems to me,
> never say "I." And that's not because they have trained
> themselves not to say "I." They don't think "I." They think
> "we"; they think "team." They understand their job to be
> to make the team function. They accept responsibility and
> don't sidestep it, but "we" gets the credit.
>
> - Peter Drucker

Max DePree says that the first responsibility of a leader is to define reality. The last responsibility, he says, is to say, "Thank you." But leaders don't wait until the end to say thanks, they say it early and often. Kouzes and Pozner write, "When nonmanagers are polled regarding the skills their managers need in order to be more effective, at the top of the list is the ability to recognize and acknowledge the contribution of others."

Regardless of who gets the credit, the impact of leadership is undeniable. Groups need leaders to achieve goals. Leadership is the catalyst that gets things going. Leadership draws out the capacity of a community. Leadership incubates the ideas that shape the future. Leadership is the aggregator that pulls the pieces together, and the glue that holds them together. Leaders create connections. They change the culture. Essentially, leaders see what needs to be done, and they do what needs to be done. The final test is whether a leader leaves behind in others the will to carry on.

LaVergne, TN USA
03 February 2010
171997LV00002B/1/P